DEALING WITH

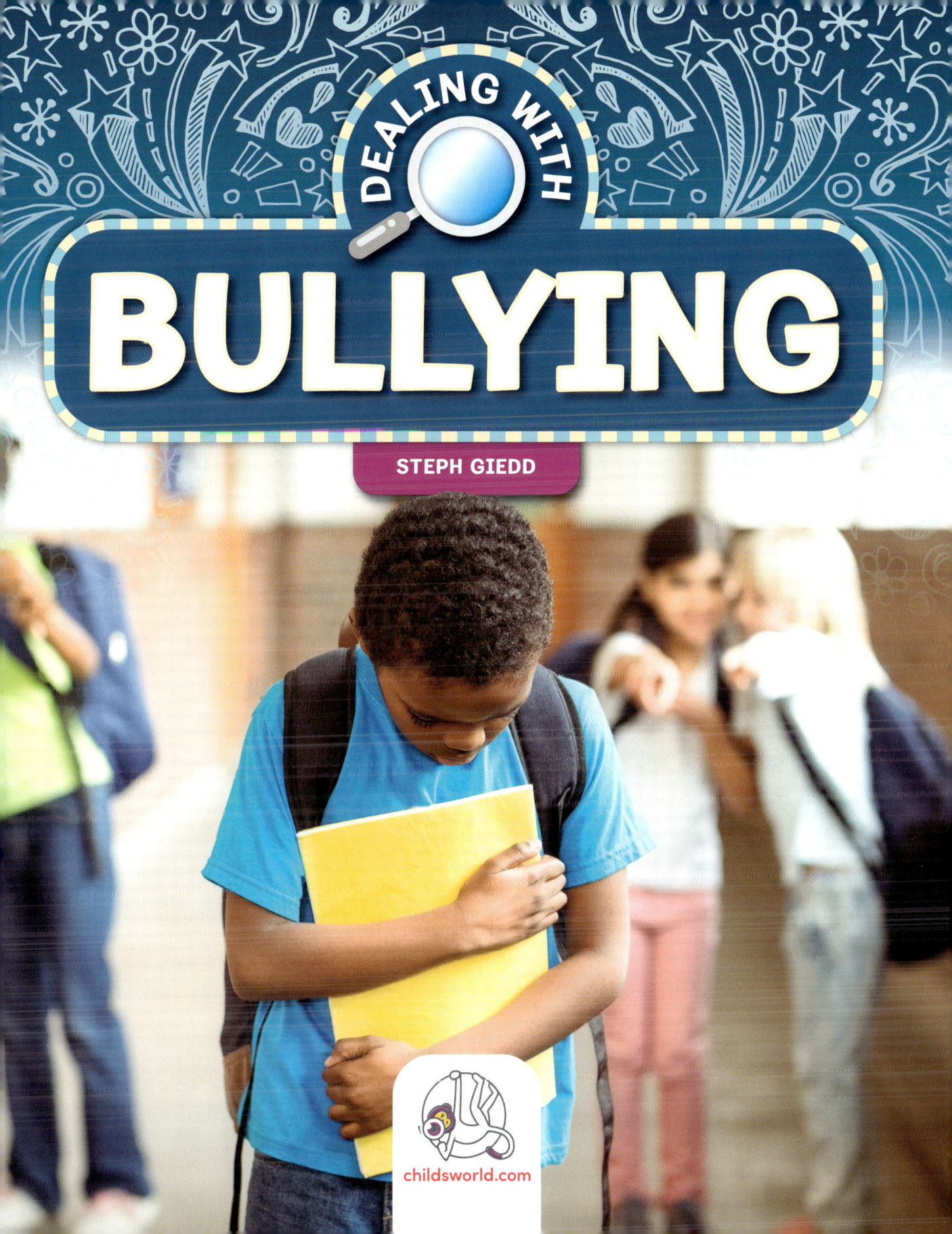

BULLYING

STEPH GIEDD

childsworld.com

Published by The Child's World®
800-599-READ • www.childsworld.com

Copyright © 2024 by The Child's World®
All rights reserved. No part of this book may be reproduced or utilized in any form or by any means without written permission from the publisher.

Photography Credits
Photographs ©: Wavebreak Media/Shutterstock Images, cover, 1; Shutterstock Images, 5, 9 (bottom left), 9 (bottom right), 12, 17, 22; Brian A Jackson/Shutterstock Images, 6; Broggi Production/Shutterstock Images, 9 (top left); Emir Memedovski/iStockphoto, 9 (top right); Monkey Business Images/Shutterstock Images, 11; Motortion Films/Shutterstock Images, 15; iStockphoto, 18; Zivica Kerkez/Shutterstock Images, 20

ISBN Information
9781503885387 (Reinforced Library Binding)
9781503885561 (Portable Document Format)
9781503886209 (Online Multi-user eBook)
9781503886841 (Electronic Publication)

LCCN 2023937460

Printed in the United States of America

Steph Giedd is a former high school English teacher who now works as an editor. Originally from southern Iowa, Giedd lives in Minneapolis, Minnesota, with her husband, daughter, and pets.

TABLE OF CONTENTS

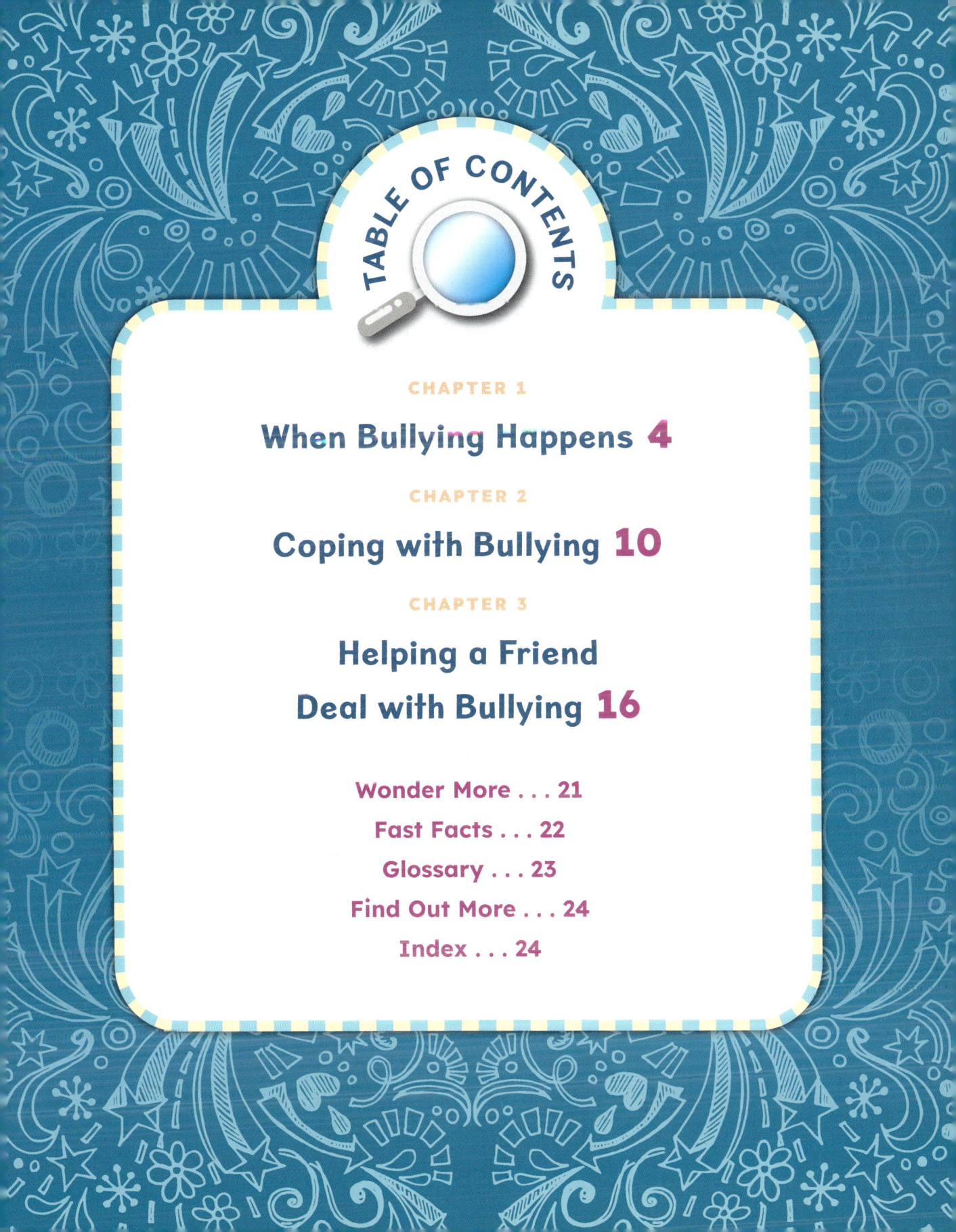

CHAPTER 1
When Bullying Happens 4

CHAPTER 2
Coping with Bullying 10

CHAPTER 3
Helping a Friend Deal with Bullying 16

Wonder More . . . 21
Fast Facts . . . 22
Glossary . . . 23
Find Out More . . . 24
Index . . . 24

CHAPTER 1

When Bullying Happens

Sometimes people are mean to others. They might pick on someone over and over. This is called bullying. People bully others in different ways. It can happen with words or actions. For example, bullies might write or say mean things about someone. Or they might pull someone's hair or hit them.

Bullying often happens in school or on the playground.

Sending hurtful texts is an example of cyberbullying.

Bullying can also happen through technology, such as computers or smartphones. This is called cyberbullying. Cyberbullying is when someone posts mean words or photos about another person online. **Social media** is one place where cyberbullying happens. It has the same effect as regular bullying. It makes the **victim** feel hurt.

One out of every five students says he or she has been bullied. It is a very common problem. Bullying can happen anywhere, not just at school. A bully doesn't have to touch or talk to someone to be hurtful. Leaving someone out of an activity on purpose is bullying as well.

Being bullied can make people feel a lot of emotions. People may feel sad, lonely, or even angry. It is OK to feel this way. These emotions might make people want to act in mean ways, too. But it is important to stay calm. People should think about how to make the situation better. There are lots of ways to deal with bullying other than being mean back to someone. Bullying is never OK. People can take action so that it does not happen again.

Effects of Bullying

Bullying can make someone feel bad about herself.

Bullying can hurt a person's relationships.

Bullying can make a person struggle to focus.

Bullying can make someone so upset she feels sick.

Bullying can hurt people in many ways. It can have negative impacts on many parts of a person's life.

CHAPTER 2

Coping with Bullying

Being bullied can be scary and hurtful. A person should try to get away from the bully. The victim can take some deep breaths. When facing a bully, it is important to stay calm. Counting to ten and focusing on breathing can help someone manage his or her emotions.

When being picked on by a bully, the victim should calmly walk away and find help.

Talking about feelings can help people feel better.

Antibullying Programs

Antibullying programs in school help make bullying happen less often. These programs include talking about bullying. Kids can learn what to do if they are being bullied. They learn why bullying is bad. Another way schools can help prevent bullying is by creating rules about it.

When people are bullied, it is important for them to not keep the painful feelings inside. They should talk to a friend or trusted adult. Parents, teachers, or guardians are often good listeners. Talking about what happened can help people **process** their emotions and get help.

Sometimes it can be hard for a person to talk about his or her feelings. Writing a note or drawing a picture may be easier. No matter how the information is shared, it is important to tell someone about the bullying. Trusted adults can help make school a safer place. They can talk to the bully. Adults can also set **consequences** if the bullying continues.

If it is safe, standing up to the bully can help, too. When bullying happens, people can take a deep breath. They can be brave and tell the bully to stop in a calm and clear voice. They can tell the bully that his or her actions aren't OK. They can also explain to the bully how it feels to be picked on. If that doesn't work, they can walk away. Sometimes, standing up to a bully isn't safe. People should not confront a bully if they are afraid of being hurt. They should tell an adult what happened and ask for help.

It is important to not be mean or hurtful back to a bully. Being mean doesn't solve the problem. If a person is mean to someone who is picking on him or her, that is still bullying. It is not OK.

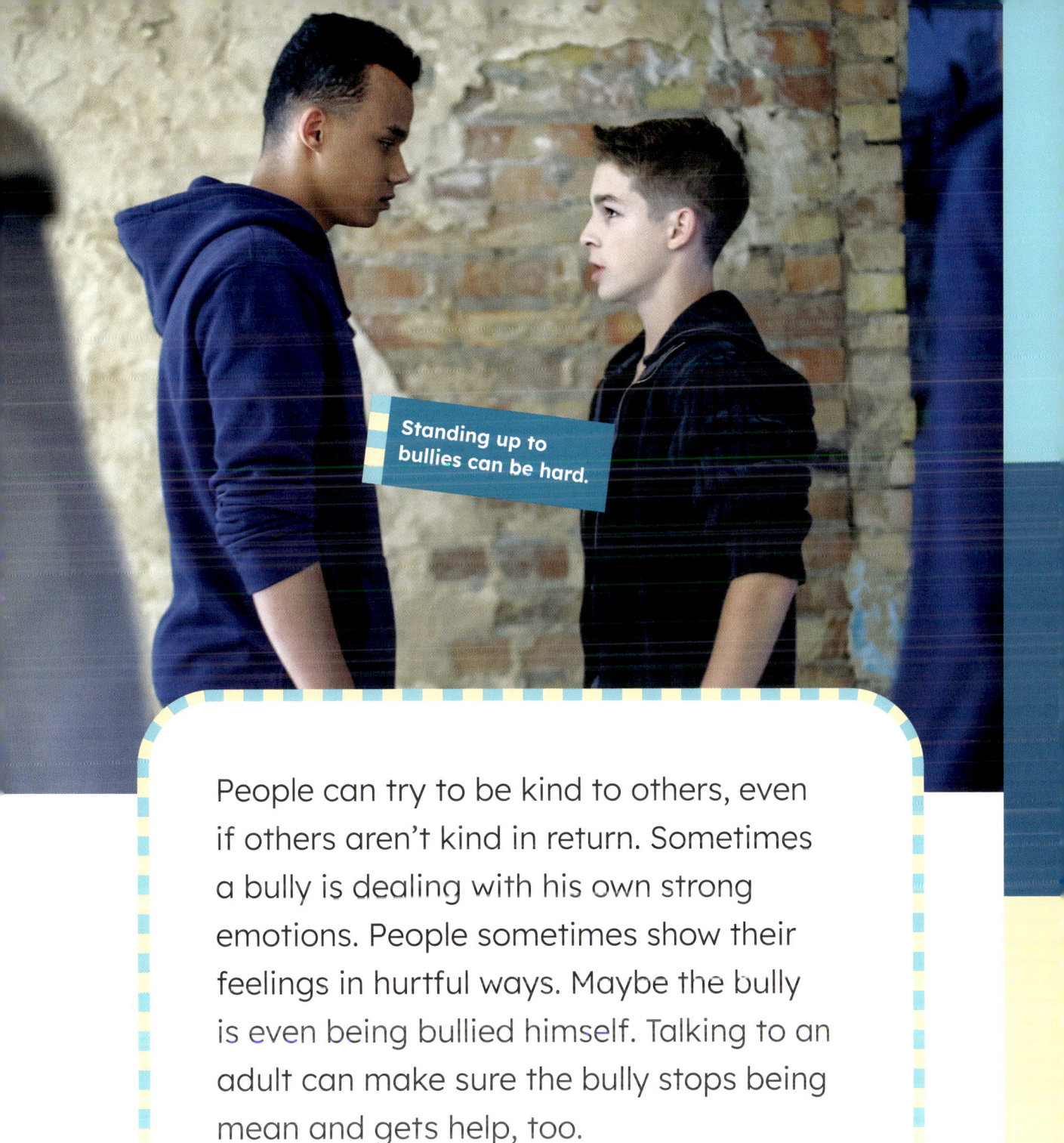

Standing up to bullies can be hard.

People can try to be kind to others, even if others aren't kind in return. Sometimes a bully is dealing with his own strong emotions. People sometimes show their feelings in hurtful ways. Maybe the bully is even being bullied himself. Talking to an adult can make sure the bully stops being mean and gets help, too.

CHAPTER 3

Helping a Friend Deal with Bullying

There are many ways to be a good friend to someone who is being bullied. First, it is important to listen. People should be there to hear their friend's feelings.

Next, they can ask if their friend wants help talking to the bully or telling an adult. Sometimes people want to handle things on their own. Other times they want support. Friends can encourage the person being bullied to stay near adults and other kids, too. A lot of times, bullying happens when others aren't around.

Good friends will always be there for others.

With a friend's help, it may be easier to tell an adult about bullying.

Bullying and Hate Incidents

A person might be bullied because of his or her race, religion, or gender. Bullies also sometimes target those who have disabilities. These are called hate incidents. Sometimes, bullying is so bad that it is a crime. Physically hurting someone because of his or her identity is one example of a hate crime.

If someone is being bullied nearby, a friend can stay and be there for her. The friend can help the victim walk away from the situation. Together, they can go tell an adult. If an adult doesn't know about the bullying, the situation could get worse. The bully will keep thinking it's OK to pick on others.

Friends can also help each other with cyberbullying. Both the person being bullied and his or her friends can **block** bullies on social media. They can also **report** bullies on the social media apps or websites. Taking a break from using social media may also help. It is important to tell a parent or trusted adult if someone is being cyberbullied. Adults don't always see what is happening online. They might not know about the bullying.

People should not just watch if someone is being bullied.

When bullying happens, it is important for people to speak up. Most kids ages nine through 12 say they are willing to help someone who is being bullied. If everyone is willing to step up, it could be a giant step toward putting a stop to bullying.

Wonder More

Wondering about New Information
How much did you know about bullying before reading this book? What new information did you learn? Write down three new facts that this book taught you. Was the new information surprising? Why or why not?

Wondering How It Matters
What is one way bullying relates to your life? If you cannot think of a personal connection, imagine how bullying might affect other kids. What impact might it have on their lives?

Wondering Why
Bullying is hurtful and not OK, but some people still do it. Why do you think some people bully others?

Ways to Keep Wondering
Bullying is an important topic to learn about. After reading this book, what questions do you have about it? What can you do to learn more about how to deal with bullying?

Fast Facts

- Bullying is when someone repeatedly hurts another person, either physically or emotionally.

- People may feel many emotions when being bullied, including sadness and anger.

- People can hurt others with what they post or write on social media. This is called cyberbullying.

- Bullying doesn't just happen at school.

- Bullying may happen when others aren't around. If someone is being bullied, he or she can try staying near adults or friends.

- Most kids are willing to help others who are being bullied.

Glossary

block (BLOK) To block someone on social media means to make that person unable to view a user's account. It is a good idea to block a cyberbully on social media.

consequences (KON-suh-kwen-sez) Consequences are the results of an action. Teachers might set consequences for bullying.

incidents (IN-suh-dentz) Incidents are events or actions. If people are bullied because of their identity, those actions are hate incidents.

process (PRAH-sess) If someone is trying to understand and deal with her emotions, she is trying to process her feelings. Adults can help victims process their emotions.

report (ruh-PORT) On social media, to report something means to say that a post or account is not following the site's rules. A user can report an account that is posting mean things.

social media (SOH-shul MEE-dee-uh) Websites where users can share information and photos are called social media. Instagram, TikTok, and Snapchat are examples of social media.

victim (VIK-tum) A victim is a person who has been hurt by an event or action. A person who is picked on is a victim of bullying.

Find Out More

In the Library

An, Priscilla. *Mindfulness with Friends.* Parker, CO: The Child's World, 2024.

Donovan, Sandy. *How Can I Deal with Bullying?* Minneapolis, MN: Lerner, 2014.

Pettiford, Rebecca. *Resisting Bullying.* Minneapolis, MN: Jump, 2017.

On the Web

Visit our website for links about dealing with bullying:
childsworld.com/links

Note to Parents, Caregivers, Teachers, and Librarians: We routinely verify our Web links to make sure they are safe and active sites. So encourage your readers to check them out!

Index

adults, 13–15, 16, 19
antibullying programs, 12

breathing, 10, 14

cyberbullying, 7, 19

effects of bullying, 7, 9
emotions, 8, 10, 13, 15

hate incidents, 18

processing emotions, 13

standing up, 14, 20

victims, 7, 10, 19